JOSHUA CHAPMANN

Building Neural Networks

Introduction to Artificial Neurons, Backpropagation Algorithms and Multilayer Feedforward Networks

JOSHUA CHAPMANN

1

information is without contract or any type of guarantee assurance.

The trademarks that are used are without any consent, and the publication of the trademark is without permission or backing by the trademark owner. All trademarks and brands within this book are for clarifying purposes only and are the owned by the owners themselves, not affiliated with this document.

Table of contents

Chapter 1 – Introduction

Neural networks are an extremely complex and vastly powerful computational technique that, over the past decade, have revolutionized the global tech industry at large. Many engineers I know repute neural networks the ***breakthrough of the decade***.

These models completely changed the way software engineers (such as myself) develop computer programs. Solving problems with NN now requires less effort and less expertise, yielding greater results. For instance, the only computer program to ever defeated a human in the extremely complex strategy game of *Go* was powered by a Neural Network algorithm.

In the past software engineers studied mathematics and statistics to produce efficient and powerful algorithms. Nowadays, they shifted their focus towards neuro biology and cognitive science to understand how our own brains work. MIT's state-of-the-art research facility, named "**Centre for Brains, Minds and Machines**", is a perfect testimonial to this fundamental interaction between the human brain and computers in today's world.

Why are engineers studying the human brain? They are not doing it for fun, medical research or some form of global engineering competition. Engineers recognized that computers can process and store much more data than humans, yet even supercomputers can't carry out tasks that the brain finds very simple such as facial recognition and natural language processing.

Hence engineers began studying the processes and structures of our human brains, hoping to build a computer model of its functions – Neural Networks were born. These are models are very simplistic, but fundamentally replicate on the inner structures of our own brains downright to the arrangement of individual brain cells, i.e. neurons.

Throughout the course of this book I will dive into the technical details and structure of neural networks. I will cover the mathematical equations and fundamental concepts that allow these models to mimic our own human brains and outperform nearly all other computer programs. In particular, I will be covering the following topics:

- How to Build a Computer model of a Brain Cell (or **Neuron**)

- The Fundamental properties of a Neural Network
- Multilayer Forward Networks
- Using the Backpropagation algorithm to learn and adapt
- Counter Propagation Networks
- How to train a Neural network (validation and testing techniques to avoid **overfitting**)

Chapter 2 – About the Series

"Neural Networks: Introduction to Artificial Neurons, Backpropagation Algorithms and Multilayer Feedforward Networks" is the second instalment of the book series **Advanced Data Analytics**, carefully developed by myself and a team of software-loving engineers. This series will provide you with a full introduction and insights into the world of modern data analytics. The material covered is roughly comparable to an undergraduate-level course in Artificial Intelligence.

Throughout the series I only assume a high-school level knowledge in mathematics and statistics and absolutely no previous exposure to computing or coding. Whenever we come across a new topic, concept or formula I make sure to cover all the required material beforehand, maximizing and facilitating your learning process.

However, my explanations can only go so far. Please understand this series will challenge and push your understanding of the modern tech world, revealing many applications of computer and algorithms you never thought possible. Especially in later books, we will dive into very technical topics at the forefront of research. To follow along and keep up with the material, I need you to be **committed** and **passionate** about the topics we will cover.

I have been working very hard on structuring the content of this series, but for now only the first publications have been officially released to the public – please stay tuned for the latest releases (my Amazon author page: ***www.bit.ly/JoshuaChapmann***). In the meantime, I would highly appreciate any feedback on the current publications and suggestions for future topics – please leave these in Amazon's official review section.

Editor's Note: The previous publication gave readers a general introduction into the world of machine learning, covering the most fundamental and popular algorithms in practice today.

If you are ready to move on, we will now dive into the world of Neural Networks.

Chapter 3 – A Brief Overview

Before we dive into the technical details of Neural Networks and how they can successfully model many aspects of our brain, I would like to provide you with a broad overview of the topic. In particular, I would like to briefly cover these fundamental questions: **what** are Neural Networks? **How** do we use them? **Why** do we use them? And **Where** do we use them?

What Are Neural Networks?

Neural Networks are immensely complex and powerful computational models built after our very own human brains. They can be used to solve extremely complex programs, but were never explicitly programmed to do so – these networks **learn how to solve problems.** Due to their complexity, I find it difficult to describe Neural Networks in a few simple words – here's my best guess:

"Neural networks are a simplified computer model of our own human brains"

In fact, on the most fundamental level our brains and neural networks do the same job: both receive input signals, process these signals and then emit an output in response. Of course there are differences in execution, but the **fundamental processes** remain the same...

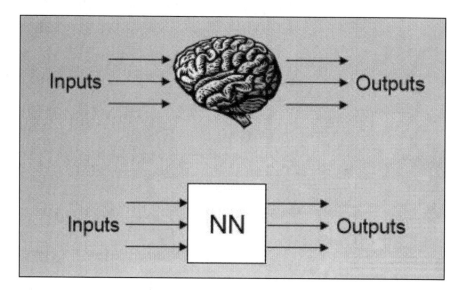

The similarities do not stop here, the structure of Neural Networks mimics our brains to a much greater degree – downright to individual brain cells. In fact Neural Networks are built using a number of *Artificial Neurons* that, just like in our real brains, are interconnected and exchange signals with one another using *synapses*.

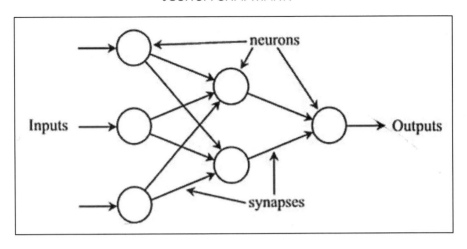

How to use Neural Networks?

"First you must train them, afterwards you can use them"

Step 1 - Training the Network: before a network can be used, it must learn how to solve problems – this occurs during training. Here is the main breakdown of the process:

1. Build a training data set (collect data samples representative of the average population)
2. **Input** the data into the network
3. The network will produce an **output** value
4. For each problem, an **error value** is calculated
5. Modify the **weights** of all artificial neurons

6. Continue training to **minimize error**
7. Once training has stopped, **test the network** to verify its accuracy

Step 2 - Using The Network: once the network has been trained correctly, solving problems is a very simple process

1. Introduce new and unseen problems
2. Let the network work through the problem (based on its training)
3. The network produces an output result

Why do we use Neural Networks?

There are two particular features that make this tool so powerful:

1. *They can learn*: In the past, when engineers were faced with a new problem they studied it, found a solution and afterwards built a program to implement the solution – with Neural Networks it's the complete opposite. Nowadays, engineers build machine capable of solving any problem and when a new problem arises the machine

studies it, learns how to solve it and only then it finds a solution.

2. *They can generalize*: Once a Neural Network learns a process, it can adapt to completely new and unexpected data. Old programs were extremely rigid – developers specify an input format and if the data does not match, then the program crashes and there is no solution. However, Neural Networks can adapt to data no one had ever seen before or search pictures nobody even knew existed.

Where do we use Neural Networks?

Neural Networks remain a relatively new technology in the industry and are yet to become mainstream. Yes, it is true that most electronics in our daily lives use machine learning algorithms, but only a few make use of Neural Networks. Most programmers believe Neural Network will work their way into nearly every piece of software within the next decade. To date, they are used in only the most advanced applications at the forefront of the tech world, including:

- Natural Language processing: ex. Google Translator
- Predicting Patterns: ex. weather forecasting

- Pattern/Facial Recognition: ex. identifying faces in videos
- Targeted search & advertising: ex. Google's search results use Neural Networks

Chapter 4 – From Deep Blue to AlphaGo

In the modern world, chess has always been a measure of intelligence and strategy between individuals. Similarly, since the invention of computers, engineers have treated this game a challenge – a battleground to prove the intelligence and power of computers.

Ever since the 1970's engineers set out to design a computer program capable of beating the chess world champion. It wasn't until 1997, that IBM's computer named *Deep Blue* achieved this task beating the reigning chess world champion Garry Kasparov. The world remained astounded at the intelligence and power displayed by computers.

Deep Blue used simple algorithms based on mathematics and statistics (such as alpha-beta pruning, tree traversal and heuristic search) to compute all the possible moves throughout the game and pick the winning combination. However, the program was so simple that you could now run it using any ordinary laptop.

However, computers have never beaten humans in the Chinese board game of **GO**. This game is immensely more complicated than chess: it is played on 13x13 boards (instead of chess's 8x8) and there are a massively greater combination of moves possible. For instance, in chess there are 20 possible first moves, while in Go there are 361.

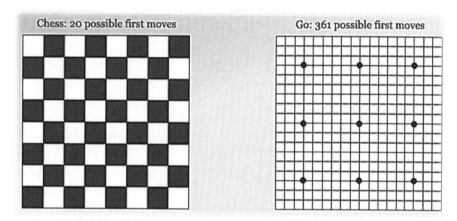

As a result of these massive combinations, even today's supercomputers are unable to predict all moves in a game and find a winning strategy. A computer program developed in 2012, using supercomputers and the most advanced algorithms to date, could only play up to beginner level. The possible combination of moves proved far too great.

With an increased attention being placed on machine learning, the AlphaGO project was finally formed in 2014. They set out to test how Neural Networks would perform in a game of GO.

The algorithm was **trained** using past games from expert human players. In other words, they showed the computer how the best humans play the game. The computer 'studied' the gameplay, recognized the best moves and 'learned' from them without any suggestions from humans. In 2016 *AlphaGO* beat the world champion in a full match. Although this achievement may not seem like much to you, it won runner-up award for the prestigious "**Breakthrough of the year**" award by *Science* magazine. This event triggered an unprecedented interest in the field. Without doubts, *AlphaGO* showcased to the entire industry the unlimited potential neural networks can deliver.

Moreover, *AlphaGO* showed that computers no longer need to be programmed to solve a problem. In the past, computers were limited by the ability of a programmer to tackle a challenge – this is no longer the case. Using Neural Networks computers can now 'observe', 'learn' from and 'adapt' to their surroundings – even better than humans do. Indeed, this issue poses a lot of questions on the future of computers and how far they will evolve and integrate within our future society.

Chapter 5 – The process of Learning

AlphaGo's success was built on one key feature: **the ability to learn**. In fact all Neural Networks share a common objective: build programs that *observe* their environments and *learn* how to solve a problem through *experimentation* and *trial-error*. In essence, we no longer program computers to carry out to a task; we create machines that can *study* a problem and afterwards *evolve* and *adapt* to solve it.

In this chapter, we will take a look at the process that makes all of it possible: *learning* and how computers can use it to solve a broad range of problems. To start this journey, we will first discuss how you and I, as humans, carry out the fundamental process *learning* and how we use this in our daily lives.

As humans, our learning instances can be traced back to a single memory or collection of memories. For instance, when I first purchased my stove I didn't know how to turn on the top-right hotplate. I opened the manual and read that to turn it on I needed to press a switch located below the command board – that was my learning experience! From that memory, I have formed a rule.

From now on, whenever I am trying to turn on the stove (**problem**) I recall the **rule** I have formed (based on **experience**) and then make an **action**. Whenever I take an action, I obtain a **feedback** on the rule's effectiveness – if the stove turns on I know the rule works, if the stove does not work I know the rule does not working and I must explore it further. This process of learning is represented in the diagram below:

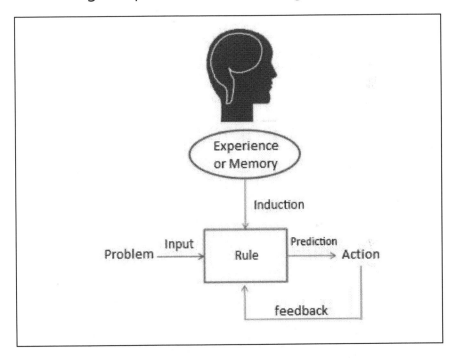

From above, we can say that our ability to learn depends on 3 parameters:

1. Amount of experiences/memories at our disposal – to help us **form** the rules

2. Amount of problems we can use – to help us **validate** & test the rules

3. Amount of feedback available with every action – to help us **improve** the rules

We have now gained a very broad understanding for how us humans learn. Let's now analyse how Neural Networks learn and respond to their environments...

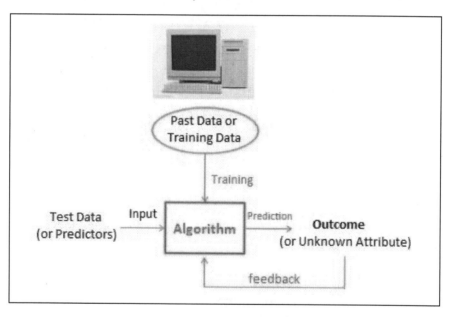

Immediately, you will notice very strong similarities between human learning and machine learning. Let's analyse the main steps & components of how Neural Networks learn in greater detail:

Training Data: this is a collection of solved examples that show the computer **how** to solve the problems (equivalent of human memories). In essence, you are providing the computer with 'memories' in the form of past, historical data. The advantage here is that you can provide the computer with a massive amount of historical, accurate data – much more than a human could ever process.

Training: this is the very essence of *learning*. During this process you run all your training data through an algorithm. This algorithm *studies* every single data point you provide, it *learns* from it and it *adapts.*

Input: Once you have trained your algorithm using historical/training data (the equivalent of memories or experiences) you are ready to test the efficacy of your algorithm (how well it has learned). You must possess the correct input & output of all your training data, but only show your algorithm the input data.

Output: Once you provide your algorithm with test data, it will make predictions and provide you with an outcome (result). Remember, you have the correct output for the test data – compare these to the results of your algorithm. Now, you can judge how accurately your algorithm performed.

Feedback: Using the test data, you now have an idea for how well your Neural Network algorithm performed. Perhaps you find out that the algorithm makes perfect predictions when provided with one type of input, but does not respond well to another type of input. In this case you must supply more training data with a particular example. Perhaps you are facing the problem of *overfitting*, meaning your Neural Network has been exposed only to a narrow range of problems and is unable to deal with new data (see chapter 12 to learn more about this problem and how you can` avoid it).

Although the process of 'learning' is presented above, there are two critical distinctions I must make before moving on: **supervised** and **unsupervised** learning.

Supervised learning

The only difference between supervised and unsupervised learning lies in the **type of training data you use**. In supervised learning you provide **labelled** training data. This means that each training example you feed into your Neural Network is classified into a recognizable data class or type. This may appear confusing, so let's walk through an example.

Think of yourself studying how to translate Spanish into English. You open a vocabulary and read that "hola" means "hello"; "manana" means "tomorrow"; "derecha" means right and so on. This data is labelled because each new input is clearly classified into a corresponding output. In other words, you clearly know how each Spanish word translates into an English word you can understand. This is supervised learning.

Unsupervised learning

As humans, unsupervised learning is a trickier concept to understand because we do it subconsciously. *Think of it as learning through observation.*

Unsupervised learning is defined by **unclassified** training data. Essentially, you provide a machine with thousands of problems and their results, but you do not explain how the results are calculated. The algorithm then starts to look for things in common; it tries to identify shared traits and features between the problems and the solutions. With enough data, the algorithm extracts a pattern and develops a strategy to solve any problem. This technique is much more powerful because it does not require human 'teaching', but requires a lot more computational power. Again, these concepts are best explained using practical examples.

Let's jump back to the revolutionary machine named *AlphaGO* – how did it learn to beat the world champion in the extremely complex Chinese game of GO? No one said 'this move is a winning move'; no one said 'follow this strategy and you will win'. These are examples of supervised learning because you are **labelling** the training data (label = 'winning move').

Instead, the engineers showed *AlphaGO* thousands and thousands of hours of expert *GO* gameplay, without labelling any move as a 'winning move' or a 'losing move'. In turn, the algorithm *observed* and *studied* all the games and it started to *understand how to play the game*. It started to spot high-level strategies and recognize scenarios. It started to understand tactics, traps and counter moves.

No one told *AlphaGO* how to play the game; they simply showed how experts already played it. Through observation, *AlphaGO* learned how to extract the best strategies and win. This is how computers use unsupervised learning to adapt and evolve, even beyond human abilities.

Chapter 6 – Biological inspiration

In the 1990's Deep Blue showed the entire world that computers could beat humans in many computational tasks. However, engineers of the time knew that even the best computers could not tackle many problems we find obvious, such as:

- Facial Recognition
- Pattern Recognition
- Natural Language Processing

These tasks are very easy for the brain, but were nearly impossible for computers to do. To gift computers with greater abilities, software engineers began to study how our brain works, how it is structured and how it processes data. Their aim was to understand exactly why it could outperform computers so easily in so many tasks – the field of Artificial Intelligence was born.

The brain proved an incredibly complex organ:

- Our brains are built by nearly **10 billion brain cells** known as neurons and possess over 60 trillion total connections.

- Each neuron had a relatively simple function consisting in receiving input (form other neurons) and emitting an output (again, to other neurons).
- When 10 billion of them are connected together, the final outcome is an incredibly complex and sophisticated processing unit unlike any supercomputer.
- The function and connection of each individual neuron changes continually – they respond to stimuli and learn to suit their environment. In essence, brains are not built they are trained.

In the 21st century, the brain represents one of the key topics for scientific research. Incredible amounts of resources and efforts are dedicated towards understanding the main functions of this organ. Unfortunately, the brain remains an extremely complex organs and we have developed all but a very rudimentary understanding of it and its function. Even the processes and behaviors of an individual neuron are extremely complex.

As always, where scientists fail to discover engineers step in to make approximations. In other words, engineers studied neural models and simplified them to obtain a realistic and above all feasible structure they could implement into computers – **Neural Networks** were born.

Engineers replaced many of the biological and chemical processes inside the brain with mathematical functions, which can easily be modelled inside a computer. Nevertheless, engineers decided to keep the same terminology as used in the field of neuroscience.

Chapter 7 – The Neuron

To understand how Neural Networks work and how they can effectively model our own brains, we must begin our journey from the most fundamental element: **the neuron**. Let's examine its structure...

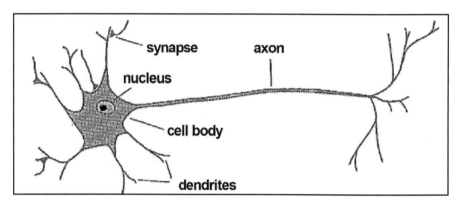

As you can tell, neurons have a main body and two branching sets of connections: the input structure (dendrites) and the output structure (the axon). The axons connect to the dendrites of other neurons via the synapse, hence forming a connection.

Signals are transmitted between neurons in the form of electro-chemical signals. A neuron first receives a signal via the dendrite to the cell body – the signal is processed, altered and assessed by the nucleus. However, the neuron will be activated only if the input signals exceed a certain amount within a short period (i.e. the threshold). If this amount is reached, the neuron becomes activated and it fires a signal to the attached neurons via the axons. This is how neurons are interconnected and exchange information.

Artificial Neurons

Now that we have a very basic understanding of a simple neuron, we can investigate how to model its functions and operation using software. We create artificial neurons as relatively simple mathematical functions – their **output** is calculated using three main factors:

- **Input signals**: these originate directly from neighboring neurons.
- **Weights**: each neuron applies a unique weighting factor to every input signal received.
- **Bias**: this value is unique to the neuron and is applied to the overall output.

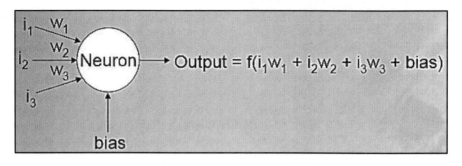

Notice that the output is not the simple sum of all the weights, it must be multiplied by an activation function. Most artificial neurons are modeled using a **sigmoid activation function**, as shown below. This is a smooth, continuous and always increasing curve (i.e. gradient is always positive). The mathematical equation of the sigmoid function is $f(x) = 1/(1 + e^{-x})$.

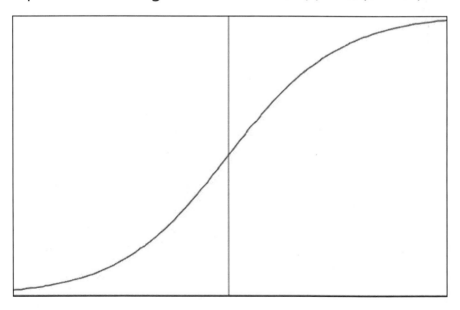

Chapter 8 – Perceptron

In this chapter we will use what we just learned about neurons and artificial neurons to build a very simple neural network – known as a **perceptron.** In fact, this network is so simple it only contains one output neuron! Nevertheless, it still exhibits the key behaviors found in today's neural networks.

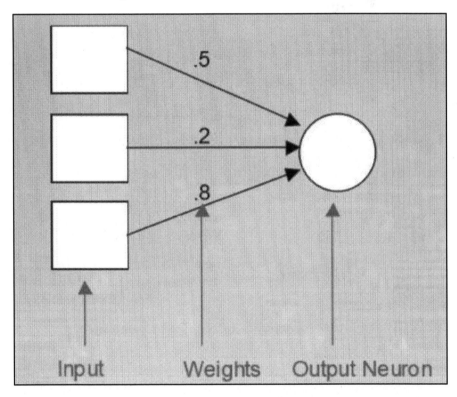

In particular, perceptrons clearly shows how artificial neurons process information and how neural networks optimize the weights in each connection to **learn**. Due to their simplicity, perceptrons have very limited applications and can only deal with relatively simple problems. I have reported the schematics of a simple perceptron below.

How Do Perceptrons Learn?

Now we are getting to the interesting bits! Let's discuss how a perceptron learns and adapts to solve a problem. Please understand we are dealing with the equivalent of a single 'brain cell' – the problems it can solve are very limited.

Perceptrons learn using supervised training, meaning you must provide a set of inputs and their matching output. The perceptron works through the input and computes an output – if it is not correct the weights are adjusted until the correct answer is obtained.

Learning is an **iterative process**, meaning individual weights must be tuned and altered repeatedly to find the most suitable combination. To find the most appropriate weights you must use the following formula:

$wt_{new} = wt_{old} + \alpha(desired - output)*input$

Where **wtnew** and **wtold** are the weights of a single connection, **α** is the learning rate (i.e. how fast a neural network adapts), **desired** is the correct output, **output** is the current output and **input** is the input value for the current connection.

This process may seem a little confusing, so let's immediately dive into an example – this will make everything much easier to understand. On the next page I have shown a fully trained perceptron (i.e. weights are already assigned) and the output is shown.

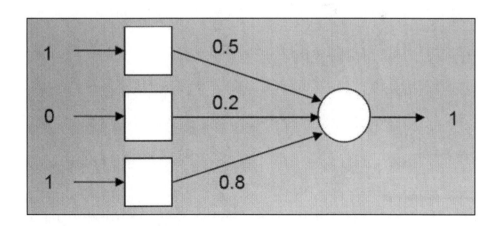

In the perceptron you will notice three inputs (1,0,1), three weights (0.5,0.2,0.8) and an output (1). Now, I want to find the weights that will produce the output value 0, how can I do this? You must follow the previous equation for each weight. Take a look below at my calculations (I have assumed α = 1 for simplicity).

Top weight:

wt_{new} = wt_{old} + $\alpha(desired - output)*input$

wt_{new} = $0.5 + 1*(0 - 1)*1$ = **0.5**

Middle weight:

wt_{new} = wt_{old} + $\alpha(desired - output)*input$

wt_{new} = $0.2 + 1*(0 - 1)*0$ = **0.2**

Bottom weight:

wt_{new} = wt_{old} + $\alpha(desired - output)*input$

wt_{new} = $0.8 + 1*(0 - 1)*1$ = **-0.2**

We have calculated new weights for the perceptron, which is now shown below. You will notice the new and updated weights are added. However, learning is an iterative process and the weights can still be tuned. As a result, we must use the activation function to calculate the new output and determine if it is satisfactory (i.e. is it close enough to our desired output?). If it is not close enough we must repeat the process above until the new output matches our desired output. This is the basis of learning in neural networks.

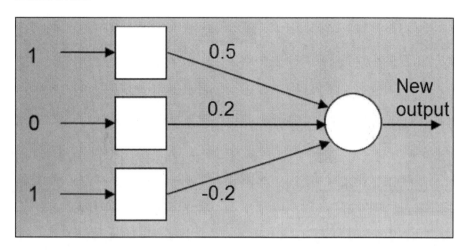

Chapter 9 – Multilayer Feedforward Networks

Multilayer Feedforward Networks (MFN) are by far the most common and widely used Neural Network architecture. They are a direct extension of the perceptrons we studied in the previous chapter and, fundamentally, work in the same way.

However, MFNs are used to solve very complex problems requiring significant computational power and cognitive abilities – these cannot be achieved using a single neuron. In fact MFNs are built using numerous artificial neurons, which are arranged in **layers**.

1. **Input layer:** these layers introduce input data and starting conditions into the network.

2. **Hidden layer**: these neurons typically perform classification base on unique and statistical features in the data. Two hidden layers are usually enough to solve most problems, without requiring excessive complexity or computationally-heavy optimization procedures.

3. **Output layer:** the result of all computations inside the network are presented to the outside world through these neurons.

The key features of this architecture are

- Information only travels in one direction(enters at input, through the hidden layer and output results are only emitted by the output layer)
- Neurons in the same layer are not attached to each other
- Hidden layers can be added or removed to easily modify computation complexity without having a major impact on the overall network

Below you can view a very basic example of a MFP with 3 layers and 5 neurons. You can see the neurons in the input layer denoted by the letter **I**, the neurons in the hidden layer are referred to using the letter **H** and the output layer neurons are referred to using the letter **O**. In this network, I have also shown examples of all weights and biases, as you would find in a real MFP.

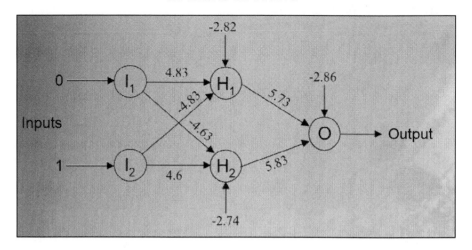

Please understand this is an extremely simple network and would only be used to solve basic, fundamental calculations. To give you a better understanding of what is used by the industry, Google uses a state-of-the-art MFP in its web search algorithms – this has **9 hidden layers**!

Chapter 10 – Backpropagation

When first building a neural network, you are essentially arranging 'blank' neurons – these have random weights and biases attached to them. Clearly, this new network cannot be used to solve problems. However, if you show it how to solve a problem it will learn how the procedure by itself. You do not need to enter any new formulas or reprogram any code, the neural network will adapt mold its functionality to your problem. Training a network to solve a problem requires minimal skill and effort, only data and time.

Backpropagation is the most common method Neural Networks use to learn. It is a critical component of all modern networks and fundamental to their widespread and straightforward implementation.

This algorithm is based on supervised training (for an explanation of supervised vs unsupervised training visit chapter 5). Meaning, in order to train a network to solve a problem you must have a set of inputs and outputs (i.e. starting conditions and the corresponding solutions).

Let's take a step-by-step look at Backpropagation and how it allows Neural Networks to learn:

Step 1 – User collects training data.

Before training the network, you must first find a set of example problems. The network will study these problems and understand exactly *how to solve the problem.* Since Backpropagation is a supervised learning algorithm, your examples must contain the input data and the correct output solution.

Step 2 – Feed input data into the network via the input layer

You must feed the input data of all your examples into the input layer of your network.

Step 3 – Network processes data to produce an output

The input data is processed by the input layer and by the hidden layer. As the signal passes through these layer, each neuron applies functions based individual weights and biases. The result is generated by the last neurons, found in the output layer.

Step 4 – Calculate the error value

For each set of input, the Backpropagation algorithm compares the actual output and the expected output. If these two values do not match, then must have been a computational error in the network – this can be quantified using the **error function**. The most common error function used is the mean squares; its formula is reported below:

Error = (correct output – obtained output)^2

Step 5 – Update neuron weights/biases & iterate!

Once the error value has been calculated, the weights and biases of every single neurons are gradually modified. First the weights and biases in the output layer are fine-tuned, working backwards into the hidden layers and finally into the input layer. This is why the learning algorithm is called 'Back'-'propagation' – tuning starts in the final layer and gradually propagates back into the network.

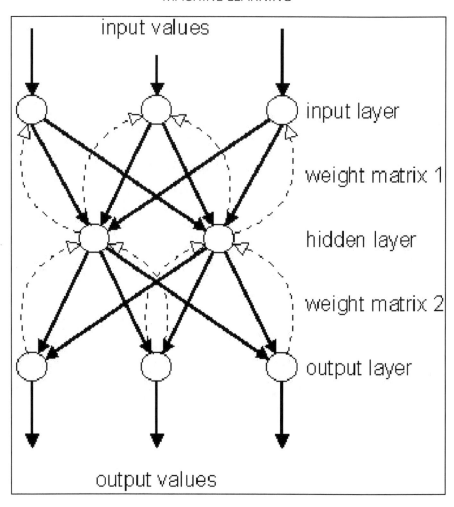

With each new weight and bias, the network's calculations are repeated and the new error is examined. Throughout all these iterations Backpropagation has only one goal: **to minimize the error function**.

Finally - Network has Learned!

Chapter 11 – Alternative Architectures

Thus far we have only covered two types of neural net structures: the **perceptron** (most basic) and **multilayer feedforward networks** (the most popular). Many different types of neural networks exist and in this chapter, I will attempt the most relevant ones.

Counterpropagation (CP) Networks

The most significant advantage of this network lies in **learning speed**: training a new CP network can be about 100 times faster than a regular multilayer feedforward network. However, once trained CP networks exhibit significantly worse **generalization** – meaning they struggle to deal with new and unseen input data, even if it's similar to the training data. In terms of structure, CP networks only contain 3 layers of artificial neurons:

- **Input layer**: as in previous structures, the neurons in this network first process the raw input data.

- **Kohonen Layer**: all neurons in this layer take a simple weighted sum of their inputs. The neuron with the largest weighted sum emits a 1 – all the other neurons emit 0.

- **Grossberg layer**: Each neuron in the Grossberg layer can receive only 1 input signal (from Kohonen layer), which is then used to calculate the final output of the network.

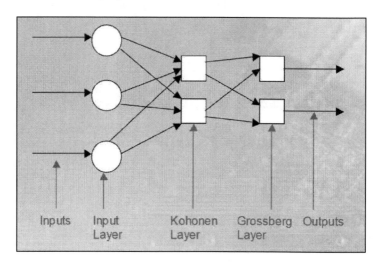

Many believe that CP networks are a better representation of the human brain than regular multilayer feedforward networks. This is because each layer in CP network operates was designed with a precise and distinct purpose. The Kohonen splits input data into separate classes and the Grossberg easily controls the network's final output using its weights (since these neurons only have 1 input signal).

Recurrent Neural Networks

Recurrent Neural Networks (RNN) are very unique – they store previous calculations and use them to improve the accuracy of future calculations. In fact, the results produced by the output layer are fed back directly into the input layer of the network.

RNN can store information about time and therefore are most suited to forecasting applications, i.e. identifying patterns in the stock market or predicting the weather.

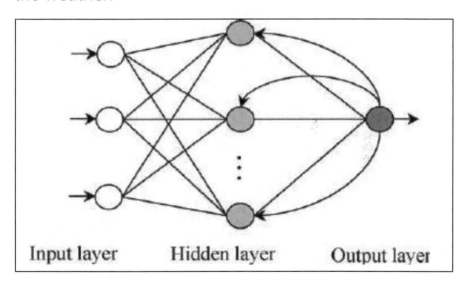

Input layer   Hidden layer   Output layer

Self-Organizing networks

Self-organizing networks use unsupervised learning and therefore can be used with unlabeled data sets.

These maps only have 2 layers of neurons: the **input** and **output** layer. These layers are essentially created 'blank' and the connections are established at a later stage. In fact, during training the network analyzes the input data and searches for statistical similarities. Based on these statistical similarities output neurons become linked to input data. In essence, this network represents a very advanced clustering algorithm.

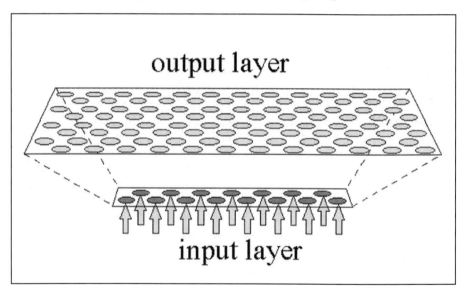

Chapter 12 – Training

Training is one of the most critical aspects of working with Neural Networks. It is extremely important you understand how to do it correctly and, in particular, what to look for when training a new network from scratch.

Overfitting

When working with any machine learning and Neural Networks in particular, overfitting is always a risk and stands to bring significant damages to the accuracy and efficiency of your models. The issue is that Neural Network are extremely powerful, perhaps even **too powerful** for their own good.

In fact, a network can often learn to mimic every detail and feature in your training data and achieve a near-zero error value – perfect, right? Not exactly - you want to build a **generalized** network that can accept and effectively work through new and previously-unseen datasets.

When a Neural Net becomes overly accustomed to your training data and is unable to deal with new previously-unseen problems, **overfitting** has occurred. This issue occurs because you did not choose a "good" training set.

Guidelines

You should never pick a training set at random – all the data should be carefully and meticulously reviewed. There are no rules you must *follow* when building a dataset, there are only *suggested guidelines*:

- Your training data should represent the general population, i.e. **typical** problems you will come across
- Your training data must contain samples from every class (or main types of problems)
- Samples in each class must cover **all possible variations**, some **unexpected inputs** and, where possible, **noise** effect.

Size

The **size** of the training data is another key aspect of training. If the set is too small you stand a high chance of overfitting, it the set is too small you may be wasting too much time training your network. The minimum size of your training data is usually dependent on the total number of neurons.

Let's consider a regular feedforward network with 4 input neurons, 10 hidden neurons and 5 output neurons. There are 90 connection weights and 19 neuron biases, for a total of **109 unknown variables**. As a general rule, the number of entries in your training data should *at least* match this number. Anything below that, you risk overfitting.

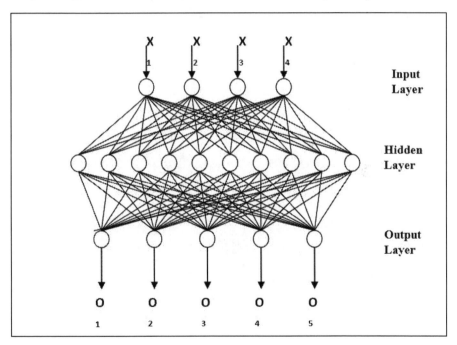

Validation and Testing

Validation and testing are the most common way to avoid overfitting; they also help us measure how well a network was trained. In fact, from all the available samples we must build 3 datasets:

- **Training Data:** this data set is used to train the network, most commonly with the backpropagation algorithm.
- **Cross Validation Data:** Cross validation data is tested during training, to ensure the network is learning appropriately and map out the error function.
- **Test Data:** Once the training stops, the final network is tested using this data set. The network solves all problems in this data set without adapting or learning, its structure has been finalized. The solution to these problems is stored and compared to the expected ('correct') solution, allowing the developers to measure how accurate the final network is.

Conclusion

Dear Readers,

I sincerely thank you for reading until this point – I hope the information in this book has proved useful and interesting.

Throughout this book we discussed Neural Networks – a particularly complex, sophisticated and yet extraordinarily fascinating type of predictive models. In fact, the structure and functions of these models is taken directly from our own human brains, which never ceases to amaze me!

We built our knowledge of these networks gradually, starting from a single artificial neuron and finally working our way up to much larger and more powerful networks, such as today's most popular choice: the Multilayer Feedforward Network. Finally, we looked at the Backpropagation algorithm and how to optimally train a network avoiding common errors, such as overfitting.

This book is also the second instalment of the **Advanced Data Analytics** series and I hope you have enjoyed it. For now, only a few books have been officially released to the public – to view all available titles, please visit my Amazon Author Page: *www.bit.ly/JoshuaChapmann*

My Most Sincere Gratitude for Reading,

Joshua Chapmann